A Passion for RED

Ellen Stern & Nancy Weber

A Welcome Book

Andrews and McMeel
KANSAS CITY

Imagine Little Green

Riding Hood or

Rudolph the Blue-

Nosed Reindeer.

Where would

mystery writers

be without

the red herring?

"A red herring is simply a false clue, something to send the detective down the wrong path. You can usually smell something fishy if the clue is so obvious that you think you've landed the culprit, only to learn later that you'll have to say, 'Holy mackerel! I've been gulled!'"

—Otto Penzler
(owner of New York's Mysterious Book Shop and purveyor of *The Red House Mystery* by A.A. Milne, *Red Dragon* by Thomas Harris, *The Red-headed League* by Arthur Conan Doyle, *The Scarlet Ruse* by John D. MacDonald, *Red Harvest* by Dashiell Hammett, "Masque of the Red Death" by Edgar Allan Poe, *Red Storm Rising* by Tom Clancy, *Red Wind* by Raymond Chandler, *Red Threads* by Rex Stout, *Crimson Joy* by Robert B. Parker, *Scarlet Letters* by Ellery Queen, *The Red Widow Murders* by Carter Dickson, *The Scarlet Pimpernel* by Baroness Orczy, and *The Five Red Herrings* by Dorothy L. Sayers.)

The Goggle-Eye:
A red fish from
the Red Sea.

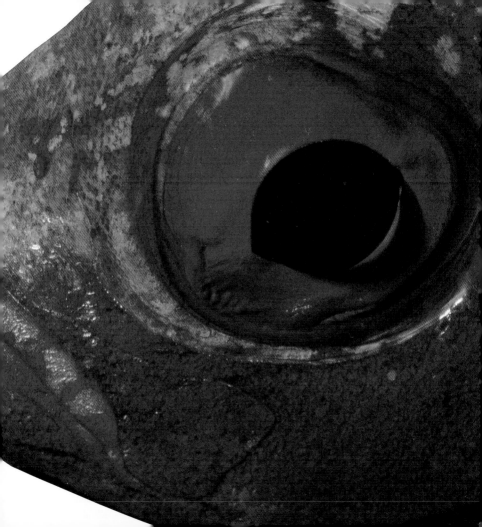

"My favorite color? Red. A lot of people are afraid to admit it, but I'm not. I've always found it to be my lucky color."

—Donald Trump

Bigwigs without
the red-carpet
treatment?

RED TIPS

Bureaucrats
without red tape?

Bicoastals without
the red-eye
special?

Santa Claus

and the

Devil

without

their

signature

suits?

"When I started making red suits for Mrs. Reagan, it was for the first inauguration: a red wool coat, a red jersey dress underneath, and a little red hat. Before that, I didn't think ladies were adventurous enough to wear red."

—Adolfo

"If you've seen one redwood, you've seen them all."

—Ronald Reagan

Man is the only animal
that blushes.
Or needs to.

—Mark Twain (a redhead),
The Tragedy of Pudd'nhead Wilson

Wild Irish Rose

If, And, But

Honey, I'm Home

K-K-K-Katie

Chuckles

For Pete's Sake

Albert's Second Car

E-Male

Lucy in Lights

Trigger Happy

Day After Tomorrow

Strawberry Charlotte

Night & Day

Instant Message

Moonlight in Vermont

Hot Flash

Oh, Bob!

On the Couch

Breakfast at Florent

One Last Kiss

e! why are you wearing those Spectacles Blue?
Here are some Glasses of Roseate Hue:
Take off the Old Pair and put on the New.
"And see if the World won't look Brighter to You.

I understand how
scarlet can differ from
crimson because I know
that the smell of an
orange is not the smell
of a grapefruit. . . .

Helen Keller, *The World I Live In*

A Chanel for Vreeland.

"Red is the great
clarifier—bright,
cleansing, and
revealing," Diana
Vreeland proclaimed
in her memoir, *D.V.*
"It makes all other
colors beautiful.
I can't imagine
becoming bored
with red—it would
be like becoming
bored with the
person you love."

Red is reds, from

Burgundy grapes

and the coral reefs

to *The Scarlet Letter*

and the

Harvard *Crimson*.

Wine, How Did You Get That Red?

It has always seemed peculiar to me that our finest red grape is called "black." The murky Pinot Noir grape produces a garnet-tinged wine with aromas of cherries, raspberries, and toasty oak. Since all the flavor and color comes from the grape skins, the trick is to capture what we want without getting too much tannin bitterness. Each fall, one-ton bins full of crushed grapes and whole Pinot berries cover the winery floor. We gently push down the cap three times a day for ten days. The back-breaking work gets more fun as the grapes ferment and scents of roses, violets, and alcohol waft up. When we consume the wine, three years later, we're buoyed by word from the medical community that the garnet liquid contains something that may help ward off heart attacks. I knew there was a reason we liked red wine.

—Deborah Cahn, Navarro Vineyard

A wine's
first duty is
to be red.

—French maxim

It is the Tuscan red

of Pennsylvania

Railroad rolling

stock, the glowing

sunset into which

a million cowboys

have ridden, and

the 15 reds in

a box of 96

Crayola crayons.

"Red Barber answered every
letter he received. He replied
on white notepad paper with his
name printed in red. He always
wrote in red ink. Red Barber was probably
our finest sports broadcaster. Red Smith of
The New York Times was probably our best
sportswriter. The two men were friends and
always addressed each other by their real
first names. Each called the other Walter."

—Bob Edwards, author of *Fridays With Red*

Shake back your hair, O red-headed girl.
Let go your laughter and keep your two
proud freckles on your chin.

—Carl Sandburg, "Red-headed Restaurant Cashier"

Hey, Red!

Woody Woodpecker

and Woody Allen,

Bricktop and

Little Orphan Annie,

Out of the ash
I rise with my red hair
And I eat men like air.

—Sylvia Plath, *Lady Lazarus*

and a host of

just Reds:

Grooms, Barber,

Buttons, Grange,

Schoendienst,

Skelton, Smith,

and Eric the.

To be red-haired is better
than to be without a head.

—Irish proverb

The first red-haired
Barbie, 1961, modeling
"Solo in the Spotlight."

UMBER !
ONTROL

POLICE

261

Who says

redheads have

less fun?

And is it

true that

red cars get

more speeding

tickets?

Red is good luck
in China,
creative
energy in
Tibet, radicalism
and rebellion from
Red Hook to the
Red Sea.

On the breast of her gown, in fine red cloth, surrounded with an elaborate embroidery and fantastic flourishes of gold thread, appeared the letter A.

—Nathaniel Hawthorne, *The Scarlet Letter*

March · 1929

THE

RED BOOK

M E

Elsie Janis
Albert Payson
Terhune
Claire Carvalho &
Boyden Sparkes
Elliott White
Springs
Rupert Hughes
William Slavens
McNutt

A
Romance
of
Wilderness Trails
and Airplanes
By William Byron Mowery

Can YOU
Make More
Money? A fascinating Test of Yourself

My Little Red Book

Three Cheers for the Red, White and Blue!

"This color has more associations, more symbolism, than any other in the spectrum—love and hate, patriotism and anarchy, sacrifice and cruelty, virtue and evil," wrote psychologist Faber Birren in *Color in Your World.*

Holly Golightly on "the mean reds"

What I've found does the most good is just to get into a taxi and go to Tiffany's. It calms me down right away, the quietness and the proud look of it; nothing very bad could happen to you there, not with those kind men in their nice suits, and that lovely smell of silver and alligator wallets.

—Truman Capote,
Breakfast at Tiffany's

"Amapola" brooch in sterling silver with red silk petals, designed by Elsa Peretti for Tiffany & Co.

SMILE WITH CONFIDENCE !
J.R. WATTS. D.D.S.
566-3636

"Oh! Grandmother,
what a terrible big
mouth you have!"

—Little Red Riding Hood

Have you seen
red today?
From sunrise
to sunset, it
suffuses the day.
It is the blush of
innocence and
the flush of
passion, as near
as the hard gloss
at our fingertips
and as remote
as the hazy call
of Mars.

China Doll

 Blue Moss

 Temple Fire

 Weeping Willow

 Joss House

 Fuchsia Blossom

 Flowering Almond

 Lotus Blossom

 Wisteria

 Opium Poppy

CHEN YU
Long-lasting Nail Lacquer

It's really <u>true</u>! The one <u>true</u> red you've spent a lifetime looking for!

"Love That Red!"

Revlon's
new-and-forever red
for lips and fingertips

Not a *pink* red, an *orange* red. a *blue* red—but a really terrific *true* red! It's a *natural*—so right for *everyone* it's become one of the *true* fashion classics of all time! Here's the one *true* red that women clamor for, year after year—and live with happily ever after!

NEW! Non-Smear-type lipstick (Same price as Revlon *regular* lipstick) 1.10*

NEW! 'Chips-Less' nail enamel .60*

'Love That Red' swimsuit by

Jantzen

*PLUS TAX

From the battlefields of the Civil War to the war on AIDS, it's the badge of courage. It is sin and salvation—the red-light district and the Red Cross, *The Red Shoes* and the ruby slippers.

Skewered through and through with office pens, and bound hand and foot with red tape.
—Charles Dickens, *David Copperfield*

Nothing in the world can
compare with red shoes!

—Hans Christian Andersen,
The Red Shoes

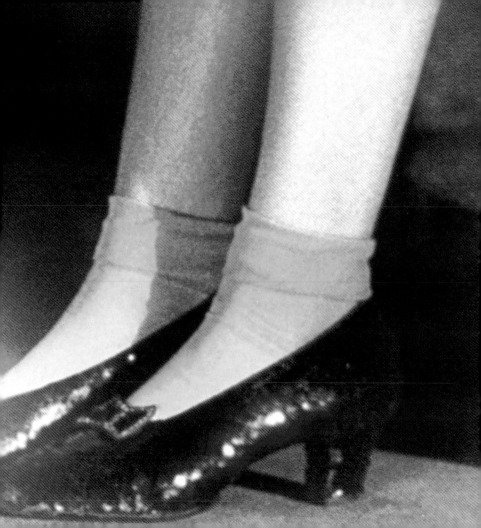

". . . And David's Lips are lockt; but in divine
High-piping Pehlevi, with Wine! Wine! Wine!
Red Wine!"—the Nightingale cries to the Rose
That sallow Cheek of hers to incarnadine.

—The Rubaiyat of Omar Khayyam,
as translated by Edward FitzGerald

With loving Greetings.

Consider

the radish,

the rose,

the redwood.

Imagine

Vivaldi, "The

Red Priest,"

gazing on

the eponymous

hues of Titian.

Red Roses

True Love

ROSES speak love ♠
The whole world through,
That is why I send ♠
Roses red to you. ♠

Think Coke and

Campbell's and

Tabasco—

and ketchup

with everything.

**The Red Lion Inn
Bloody Mary**
1 ounce vodka
3/4 cup tomato juice
2 dashes lemon juice
4 dashes Worcestershire sauce
2 to 3 drops Tabasco sauce
2 dashes salt and pepper
1/4 teaspoon horseradish (optional)
fresh celery stick, for garnish
lime wedge, for garnish

"I don't care for the pale people; I like them
with lots of blood in them. . . ."

—Bram Stoker, *Dracula*

Why is the sky blue?

Why is red red?

What IS red?

A physicist will

sing of wavelengths.

Yes, but.

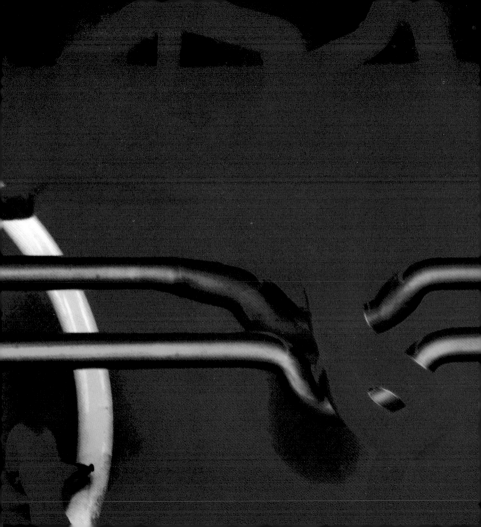

A small boy

yearns after a

red balloon

If one says "Red" (the name of a color)
and there are 50 people listening
it can be expected that there will be
50 reds in their minds.
  And one can be sure that all those reds
will be very different.

because the

  Even when a certain color is specified
which all listeners have seen
  innumerable times—such as the red of the
Coca-Cola signs which is
  the same red all over the country—they will
still think of
  many different reds.

eye has reasons

  Even if all the listeners have hundreds
of reds in front of them
  from which to choose the Coca-Cola red,
they will again select
  quite different colors. And none can
be sure that he has found
  the precise red shade.

that reason

cannot know.

—Josef Albers, *Interaction of Color*

In olden days, a glimpse of

flannel was held to have

curative powers, as long as it

was red and you wore it

close to your heart.

IF YOU WANT A
VALENTINE,
JUST HAVE ME
PAGED.

And she ate of the fruit
of the pomegranate tree
and she knew that she
was naked.

—Nancy Werd, *PersephonEve*

New Age healers

would have

you gaze on

red instead.

Is the redness of

cherry-flavored

cough syrup part

of the cure?

Better red . . .

OH YOU LOBSTER!

. . . than dead.

And when the

, red, red robin

A ball of fire shoots through the tamarack
In scarlet splendor, on voluptuous wings

—Joel Benton, *The Scarlet Tanager*

comes bob,

bob, bobbin'

along, it might

as well be spring.

A robin redbreast in a cage
Puts all Heaven in a rage.

—William Blake, *Auguries of Innocence*

"Tendresse," steel sculpture
by Mark di Suvero

Be my valentine

Let's paint the

town red.

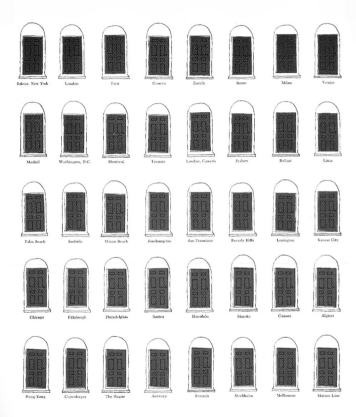

Salens: New York · London · Paris · Geneva · Zurich · Rome · Milan · Venice

Madrid · Washington, D.C. · Montreal · Toronto · London, Canada · Sydney · Belfast · Lima

Palm Beach · Surfside · Miami Beach · Southampton · San Francisco · Beverly Hills · Lexington · Kansas City

Chicago · Pittsburgh · Philadelphia · Boston · Honolulu · Biarritz · Cannes · Algiers

Hong Kong · Copenhagen · The Hague · Antwerp · Brussels · Stockholm · Melbourne · Matson Line

Around the world in forty doors
that's the beauty of *Elizabeth Arden*

Something just-

struck me

For information write:
Andrews and McMeel
A Universal Press Syndicate Company
4900 Main Street
Kansas City, Missouri 64112

A Welcome Book
Welcome Enterprises, Inc.
575 Broadway
New York, New York 10012

Design by Timothy Shaner

Library of Congress Catalog Card Number: 95-77550

ISBN: 0-8362-0801-3

Printed in China by Toppan Printing
10 9 8 7 6 5 4 3 2 1

ILLUSTRATION CREDITS **Page 3:** Reprinted by permission of the New England Aquarium; photo by Paul Erickson. **Pages 6–7:** Courtesy of the Ronald Reagan Presidential Library. **Page 7:** (bottom right) Photo by Christopher Measom. **Page 11:** (right) Courtesy of the Metropolitan Museum of Art; photo by Karin Willis. **Pages 12–13:** Jell-O® is a registered trademark of Kraft Foods, Inc. **Page 14:** (left) Illustration by Peter Stern. **Page 18:** (inset top) Texaco Fire Chief © 1992 Texaco Inc., reprinted with permission from Texaco Inc.; (inset bottom) Sheet music courtesy of Sandy Marrone; Mobil photo © John Margolies, 1980. **Page 23:** (left) Barbie courtesy of Mattel Toys; (right) Sheet music courtesy of Sandy Marrone. **Page 26:** (bottom left) Sheet music courtesy of Sandy Marrone; (right) *Redbook* cover reprinted by permission of *Redbook* magazine © 1929 by the Hearst Corporation. All rights reserved. **Page 28:** Photo by Lee Fox. **Page 29:** (left) Courtesy of Tiffany & Co. **Pages 30–31:** 1959 Mack Searchlight fire truck from the Collection of the New York City Fire Museum, photo by Michael Boucher. **Page 32:** (top) Photo by Roz Joseph. **Page 35:** Courtesy of Revlon Consumer Products Corporation. **Page 36:** (bottom right) "Red Ribbons" for the American Federation for AIDS Research, courtesy of Angotti, Thomas, Hedge: Frank Guzzone and Ken Sandbank, photo by Bruce Barnbaum/Swanstock. **Page 37:** Everett Collection. **Pages 38–39:** from *The Wizard of Oz* © 1939 Turner Entertainment Co. All Rights Reserved. **Page 42:** (right) Courtesy of Campbell Soup Company. **Page 43:** (bottom right) Illustration by Peter Stern. **Pages 44–45:** Photo by Lee Fox. **Page 46:** "Coca-Cola" and the contour bottle are trademarks of The Coca-Cola Company. **Page 47:** *Homage to the Square* by Josef Albers courtesy of the Josef Albers Foundation. **Page 49:** (top) "February," photo by Nora Scarlett. **Page 50:** (right) "Pomegranates," photo by Carol Kaplan. **Page 51:** Photo by Lee Fox. **Page 52:** Swiss Champ Original Swiss Army Knife from Victorinox. **Page 53:** (left) Courtesy of Heinz U.S.A. **Pages 54–55:** © The Walt Disney Company. **Page 57:** (right top to bottom) Courtesy of The New Era Hat Company. **Page 58:** (right top) Photo by George Bellamy. **Page 59:** (right) Courtesy of Elizabeth Arden. **Pages 62–63:** Courtesy of Driscoll Strawberry Associates, Inc. **Page 64:** Courtesy of the New York City Department of Transportation; photo by Jayne Pagnucco.